PRAYER OF THE FAITHFUL
FOR VARIOUS OCCASIONS

PRAYER
of the
FAITHFUL

For Various Occasions

VERITAS

Published 2013 by
Veritas Publications
7–8 Lower Abbey Street
Dublin 1, Ireland
Email publications@veritas.ie
Website www.veritas.ie

ISBN 978 1 84730 515 2

10 9 8 7 6 5 4 3 2

Cover designed by Heather Costello, Veritas
Printed in the Republic of Ireland by Anglo Printers Ltd, Drogheda

Preface

This booklet seeks to help you in devising prayers of intercession for the Prayer of the Faithful in various occasions. You may use the prayers as they stand or draw from them inspiration when writing your own.

Contents

Introduction   9

Invitation to Prayer   11

Weddings   13

Christenings   17

    General   17

    After the Baptism of an Adult   18

    Prayers for Mothers   19

    Prayers for Fathers   20

Funerals   21

    General   21

    For One Who Has Died Because of Illness   25

    For Carers   26

    For a Child Who Has Died   27

    For One Who Has Died by Suicide   28

    Month's Mind   30

    Anniversary Mass   31

    Intercessions for Healing   32

Anniversaries   33

    Silver/Golden Wedding Anniversary   33

    Golden Jubilee   34

    Celebration of Priesthood   35

Students and Schools   37

    General School Mass (Primary)   37

    General School Mass (Secondary)   38

    For the Beginning of the Primary School Year   39

    For the End of the Primary School Year   41

    For Confirmation Enrolment   43

    For the Beginning of the Secondary School Year   44

    For First Years in Secondary School   45

    For the End of the Secondary School Year   46

    For Exams   47

Stations   49

General Intercessions   51

    General   51

    For the Church   52

    For Christian Unity   53

    For Before Meetings   54

    For the Environment   55

    For New Drivers   56

    For the Alleviation of Stress   57

    For a New Home   58

    For John Paul II   59

    For John XXIII   60

Closing Prayers   61

Introduction

This booklet lists intentions for prayers of intercession that may be used as they stand or may be adapted for the Prayer of the Faithful.

Usually, five to six intentions are read. In determining the content of the Prayer of the Faithful, it should be kept in mind that intercessions may be made for the Church, for civil authorities, for those oppressed by various needs, for the salvation of all humanity, as well as for the specific intention of the Mass, be it wedding, funeral etc.

The structure is simple: the priest begins with an opening invitation to prayer and the reader(s) read(s) the intentions, followed by a common prayer response or invocation. The priest then says a closing prayer.

While the people's prayer in the form of a response may be composed for the occasion, there are a number of standard invocations:

> Lord, hear us. *Lord, graciously hear us.*
> Let us pray to the Lord. *Lord, hear our prayer.*
> We pray to the Lord. *Lord, hear our prayer.*
> Lord, in your mercy. *Hear our prayer.*
> Lord, have mercy. *Lord, have mercy.*

Some moments of silence should also be included.

Invitation to Prayer

In our need, we pray:

The Lord is good and forgiving, full of love to all who call. Let us present our needs before the Lord with confidence.

We present our petitions to the Lord of justice, confident that our cry will be heard.

We present our needs before the Lord, confident that the Lord of compassion, who cares for his people, will hear.

'I am the saviour of all people,' says the Lord. 'Whatever their troubles I will answer their cry.' Let us present our petitions to the same Lord with confidence.

Saint Paul encourages us to offer prayers for everyone. With this in mind, let us present our needs before the Lord.

As people of faith we stand before the Lord to present our needs, confident that we will be heard.

The love of Christ gathers us together in communion so that we might be renewed through this celebration of our faith and in our commitment to bring the Gospel to the ends of the earth, and so we make our prayer to our loving Father.

The Lord hears the cry of the poor; we present our petitions before the Lord, confident that he will hear and answer.

Weddings

For N. and N., that the Lord, who has brought them to this happy day, will keep them forever in fidelity and love.

For the parents of N. and N., for their friends, and for all who have helped them in preparation for this day.

For the world and its peoples, that the Lord may bless them with his peace and the protection of his love.

For our community and our families, who welcome Christ into their lives, that they may learn to receive him in the poor and suffering people of this world.

For God's Church, the Bride of Christ, that it may be united in faith and love.

For all who are victims of injustice, and for those deprived of love and affection.

For married couples everywhere, that their lives will be an example to the world of unity, fidelity and love.

For those who mourn, while we are rejoicing, that in their suffering and loneliness they may experience the strength of God's support.

For the faithful departed and especially for those whom we ourselves have loved, that God will one day unite us again in the joys of our eternal home.

For N. and N., that their love for each other may continue to grow in the peace of Christ.

For N. and N. who now celebrate with us their joy and gratitude in receiving God's gift of love in the Holy Sacrament of Matrimony; that they may grow old together by sharing life's joys, struggles and challenges in order to become better persons and Christians. May the blessings of the Lord guide them through their lives as husband and wife.

For all married couples here today, that witnessing N. and N. making their commitment of love, they renew their love for one another.

For the parents of N. and N., who have given much of themselves to raise their children in the way God intended, that he may bless them with good health and peace of mind.

For the family, relatives and friends of N. and N., who have been there to support them through the years, that God may bless them with love and peace always.

For all that are gathered here today to celebrate with N. and N., especially those who have travelled a great distance, that God will bless them and watch over them.

For the deceased relatives and friends of N. and N., that God may shower them with eternal love.

For the Holy Church and her leaders, Pope Francis, our Bishop N., and all our bishops, clergy and religious, that by their words and witness they may continue to build God's kingdom of justice, peace and unity.

Taken from *A Wedding of Your Own* by Pádraig McCarthy (Veritas, 1988); *On the Way to the Wedding* by Elizabeth Hughes (Veritas, 2000); and *Distinctive Weddings* by Bláithín O'Reilly Murphy (Veritas, 2006).

We pray that the love of bride and groom may grow deeper each day, and may that love strengthen and comfort them on their journey through life together.

We pray for the parents of the bride and groom, for all their family and friends, both present and absent. May their love and friendship be a constant source of inspiration and support to the bride and groom in the years ahead.

We pray for our deceased relatives and friends. We thank God for the happy memories they have left with us. Bless them and keep them in your care, and may God one day unite us in the joys of our eternal home.

For all those who suffer injustice and hardship in the world, and for those deprived of love and affection, that they may someday find peace through God's love.

Christenings

General

For the gift of life, as we thank God for the new life and gift of N..

We pray that the Angel of Peace be a faithful guide and friend to N..

We pray for God's forgiveness of all our sins and offences.
May the gift of life be an example of how we can live as good Christians.

We pray for the Church and all her members, that God will grant peace, protection and unity.

We pray for our families and friends who will be an example to N.. May they grow in wisdom and knowledge of God's love.

We pray for all babies who are now angels in the house of God.
May God continue to care for and protect them.

After the Baptism of an Adult

We pray for the Church and all who serve it. May God bless and protect all her members.

We pray for N. as he/she has made this faithful decision to become a member of the Church. May he/she be a faithful follower and witness to the Gospel.

We pray for all the people who have accompanied N. on this journey. May they always be faithful and committed to the Gospel and may God bless them for their time and generous hearts.

We pray for all who are gathered here today. May the renewal of their baptismal vows bring light and goodness to each of their lives.

We remember N.'s family and all the people who have gone before us. May God always keep them in his love.

Prayers for Mothers

We pray for all mothers. May they, like Mary, show their children the extent of human love and motherly nurturing, and may all people learn to embrace one another in love, compassion and service.

As your servant, Mary listened. May all mothers be open to your plans for us with a listening heart and respond with a generous spirit.

May Jesus, born of an ordinary woman, Mary, hold all mothers close to his heart and grant his blessings.

Mary rejoices in heaven. We pray for all mothers who are now rejoicing in eternal life.

Prayers for Fathers

We pray for all fathers. May the love of God the Father be a great example to all.

We pray that all fathers will be like St Joseph, that they will always stand by their children and be examples of faith so their children can grow to be faithful followers of the Lord.

May Jesus, brought up by an ordinary man, Joseph, hold all fathers close to his heart and grant his blessings.

We pray for all fathers who are no longer with us. May they enjoy their heavenly home and continue to look over their children.

Funerals

General

We pray for N.. In baptism he/she was given the pledge of eternal life. May he/she now be admitted to the company of the saints.

We pray in thanksgiving for all the blessings that came to so many people through the life of N.. May he/she now receive the fullness of God's blessings in eternity.

God, you are full of mercy and compassion. Forgive N. any sins he/she committed through human weakness.

N. touched all our lives. Help us to keep alive the values and the ideals he/she put before us.

We pray for all our departed brothers and sisters. Today we pray for ... May N. be reunited with them in God's kingdom where there is no more pain or suffering.

We pray for the family and friends of N.. In these difficult days may the Lord be their strength and their consolation.

May the God of all consolation be with all who are in sorrow and mourning the loss of N.. May he give them the courage and strength to live through this time of suffering which has been laid upon them and bring to them a deep peace, which only he can give.

Today we are saddened by the loss of one whom we have loved. May our hope in the Resurrection and the promise of eternal life bring us comfort and turn our sadness to joy.

We pray for all who are gathered here in worship. May our own lives bear witness to the generous love of the Lord who lived, died and rose from the dead so that we may have life and have it to the full.

May the God of all consolation help us in our grief to comfort one another. May we find light in time of darkness and faith in time of doubt.

We pray for all our deceased relatives and friends. May the Lord bring them into the light of his presence and give them a share in his glory.

We pray for all who are suffering with ill health at this time. May they experience the loving kindness of the Lord in and through all who journey with them.

We ask the Lord's blessings on all those who are seriously ill. Be close to them in their time of sickness, and if it be your will, heal them and restore them to full health again.

We remember today those who are terminally ill. May the Lord be close to them as they enter into the last stage of their journey towards their homeland.

Taken from material collated by St John the Baptist Church, Clontarf.

Let us pray for N.. In baptism he/she died with Christ, may he/she now share in the fullness of his Resurrection.

God is full of mercy and compassion. May he forgive N. any sins he/she committed through human frailty.

For the sorrowing family, relatives and friends of N., that you may find strength and consolation in your Christian faith and in the love and support of this community.

We pray for those who mourn N.'s death (especially ...), that you may find strength and consolation in the hope we have through the Resurrection of Jesus from the dead.

God of all consolation, help us to comfort one another in our grief, finding light in time of darkness, and faith in time of doubt.

We pray for all those we have loved who have died. Lord, give them the reward of their goodness.

We pray for those who care for the sick and dying, especially those who cared for N. during his/her illness.

For all parents who grieve over the death of their children, that they may be comforted in the knowledge that they rest in God.

May the prayers of Mary, the Mother of God, who stood by the cross as her son was dying, help those who mourn and be with all of us in our time of need.

We pray for those here today, that our memory of N., whom we loved, inspires us with a renewed love for all our sisters and brothers.

We pray for all of us here today and for all members of our Church, that we may be prepared for the hour of our death, when God will call us by name, to pass from this world to the next.

Taken from http://www.ballyroanparish.ie/funerals/readings-for-funeral-masses/prayers-of-the-faithful and http://kingscourtparish.ie/bereavement/general-readings-prayers-of-the-faithful/; accessed 27 August 2013.

For One Who Has Died Because of Illness

We thank God for all the special times we enjoyed with N. and we ask God to welcome N. into your kingdom to enjoy perfect peace.

We pray for all our departed loved ones at this time, especially ...

We ask God to bless all who cared for N., especially ...

We pray for N.'s family. May God comfort them and support them during this time and during the tough times ahead. We ask you to bless N.'s friends and their families and all who supported N. with their love during his/her illness.

We pray that the medical research teams will find a cure for all life-threatening illness.

We pray that N. will be happy with the Lord and will find peace and love in his/her new heavenly home and continue to watch over us.

For Carers

We pray for all who care for the sick at home or in hospital. May God bless them with patience and compassion in their ministry of healing.

We pray for those who offer spiritual support to the dying and to their families. We ask God to grant them strength and understanding in their work of pastoral care.

We pray for those who support hospice care and all the work they do. We ask God to empower them to continue to offer dignity and respect to all who are on their final journey in their mission of mercy.

We pray for the cure of cancer. May the medical experts be guided by the Holy Spirit in their work.

We pray for all who care for patients, that God will continue to guide them and stay with them and support them as they care for their loved ones and patients.

For a Child Who Has Died

We pray for the parents of beloved N.. May God comfort and protect them and help them find peace. May renewed hope be rekindled in God's love and the love of all who support them.

We pray for N.'s brothers and sisters. May they be protected and comforted by God's love and have the gift of understanding and courage in their lives.

We pray for the grandparents, aunts and uncles and all family members of N.. May they too be comforted and consoled.

We pray for all who care for the sick, and especially those who care for sick children, for the doctors and nurses who took care of N. so well and all who help families to cope at the time of sickness.

We pray for all families who have lost a child. May God bless them and fill their hearts with his love.

We pray for everyone who has come today to say goodbye to our beloved N.. We thank God for their support and presence.

For One Who Has Died by Suicide

We pray today for N.. Though his/her time with us has tragically been cut short, may he/she find peace and love in the Father's heavenly home.

We pray especially for N.'s family. May God comfort and console them, and keep them in his loving care.

We remember today all who have died by suicide, now resting in the arms of God's compassion and love.

We pray for all who are anxious, lonely and depressed. May they know that there is always hope, and may God's healing hands bless and protect them.

We pray for all who care for and support those with mental health issues. May there be more awareness and support, and may God guide, direct and encourage all who work in this area.

We pray in thanksgiving for our family members, and all those who have gone before us.

We pray for each person gathered here, that we may continue to serve and share the love of Christ with all we meet.

We remember those who have taken their own lives. May they come to know the compassion and love of God.

We ask the Lord to stay close to those bereaved by the suicide of someone they love. May they meet Christ in the love and support of other people as they endeavour to cope with the struggle and loss.

We pray that the spirit of hope will dwell in us all. May the God of compassion open our ears and eyes to each other and may the light of Christ shine in the dark places of our lives.

We remember today all here present who are deeply saddened by the unexpected passing of their loved one. In the days, weeks and months ahead, we ask the Lord to give each of them great courage to bear this huge loss together, giving each other a listening ear through their kind presence at this difficult time.

Month's Mind

We pray for N. and remember him/her in a very special way today, giving thanks for his/her life and for the memories we have.

We pray that N. has reached the safety of God's everlasting and loving home.

We pray that N. is now united with all his/her loved ones and friends. May peace and joy be with them all.

We pray for everyone here today, especially the family and friends of N.. May they receive the help and support they need.

We pray for all who mourn for their loved ones. May they receive comfort and hope.

We pray that we will continue to live well and fully in this life. May we have hope in the life to come and one day share it with our loved ones who have gone before us, especially N..

Anniversary Mass

We pray that Jesus, who is the Resurrection and the Life, gives peace to all who have died.

We pray for all who have died this year, especially N., whose anniversary now occurs – may they be welcomed into the communion of saints, and share in the joy of heaven.

We pray for all the bereaved and sorrowing, especially the family of N.. May they find comfort in the belief that death has no power over their loved one.

We pray that the Risen Lord may be our guide and support as we journey through life, through death, and to life eternally.

Intercessions for Healing

We ask our loving God to lay your healing hands on all who suffer with pain and poor health.

We ask our loving God to take care of all who suffer in mind and spirit. May they know the presence of your love and protection.

We ask our loving God to hold in your loving arms all who suffer in our world because of injustice and violence.

We ask our loving God to bring the gift of wisdom to all who struggle with addiction, and to help and continue to guide those who support and work with them.

Loving God, we are conscious of the suffering of your creation. May we all have the gift of knowledge to help protect your creation.

Loving God, we remember all who are bereaved and suffering from a loss. Grant them your peace and fill their hearts with the presence of your love.

Anniversaries

Silver/Golden Wedding Anniversary

We pray for all married couples. May God keep them faithful to him and stronger every day in their love for each other.

We pray for N. and N. on this joyful occasion and for the gift of love and happiness their marriage has brought. May God continue to grant them happiness in their love for each other.

We pray that N. and N. will continue to be an example to all who are united in the sacrament of marriage.

We pray for the family of N. and N. and we give thanks for the gift of family life. May we never take for granted the love we have received and may we be thankful always for God's blessings.

We pray for all who have gathered here today. May the gift of friendship be ever more closely united through this celebration of love and joy.

We pray for the sick, the bereaved and especially married couples who have not had the chance to celebrate their silver/golden anniversary. May the Lord keep them in his loving care.

We pray for all the deceased members of N. and N.'s family, especially ... May they continue to enjoy the happiness of eternal life, until we meet again.

We thank God for this indescribable gift of love. Help us to share and receive your love with all we meet.

Golden Jubilee

We thank the Lord for the gift of N., by whose inspiration we have been graced with so many sisters/brothers/priests in their ministry of education/caring.

We remember the parents, siblings, and other relatives and friends, mentors and colleagues of N., who have supported N. all these years as he/she walked the path of his/her vocation.

We gather in our prayer the many people, old and young, whose lives N. has touched by his/her untiring and selfless love for all.

We pray that N. continues to live his/her life in the Lord with peace of mind and compassion.

We pray that N., with the assistance of Our Lady and the Holy Spirit, continues to represent the Church in our modern world.

Celebration of Priesthood

We pray for N. and his [number] years of priesthood. We thank God for the blessings given to him.

We pray for N.'s family and friends, who have supported him throughout his ministry.

We pray for the sick, the bereaved and all those who face challenges.

We pray for vocations to the priesthood and religious life.

We pray for all our deceased, especially … May they enjoy the happiness of eternal life.

Students and Schools

General School Mass (Primary)

We pray for all who care for us; the staff of our school, our parents, grandparents and our families.

We pray for our teachers; that they may continue to help us be the best that we can be.

We pray for children everywhere; that their homes and schools are places where they know that they are loved and cared for always.

We pray for all who have died; we remember especially grandparents and all those we loved. May they be at peace with God in his heavenly home.

Taken from http://stoliverscarlingford.scoilnet.ie/blog/files/2012/01/CSWWednesdayPart2.pdf; accessed 27 August 2013.

General School Mass (Secondary)

For our school community: we pray today for all of us gathered here. May we always be open to receive your light and love so that our school can be a living example of faith in action. May we be true to the heritage of N. [our founding congregation] and the inspiration of N. [name of the founder].

For leadership: we pray for the leaders of our country, our community and our Church. We pray especially for the leaders here in our own school community: our board of management, our principal and deputy principal, our teachers and our student council. May they always make decisions based on justice and respect for the dignity of the human person.

For those who struggle with their faith: we pray today for those people who struggle to find God in the world around them, for those who find it hard to believe in a loving God. May the Lord help them to feel the light of your guiding and comforting presence in their lives and help us to deepen our faith in your presence.

Martin Luther King once said that everything which is done in the world is done by hope. There is much to be done in our world today. May the God of love help us to face with resilience and courage the challenges and promises of the life which you have given us.

Taken from http://www.lecheiletrust.ie/prayers/91-prayer-service-for-catholic-schools-week; accessed 27 August 2013.

For the Beginning of the Primary School Year

We thank God for bringing us together and we pray for a good year at the beginning of our new school year.

We pray that God will help us work hard at our school work. May God bless all the work we do.

We pray that we will have lots of fun together and that we will never leave anyone out. May God bless all the games that we play.

We pray that we will use all the lovely gifts that God has given us. May we always be thankful for all our wonderful gifts.

We pray that we will always be good friends to each other and take care of each other.

We pray that God will bless all our teachers. May we always listen to them and be kind to them.

We pray for our families and we ask God to keep them safe.

We ask God to bless our school, teachers and everyone who works here.

May God bless the work that we do, help us to grow in knowledge and understanding.

May God bless the games that we play, help us to grow in strength and fairness.

May God bless the things we create, help us to grow in imagination and joy.

May God bless the time we spend together, help us to grow in harmony and peace.

May God bless the time we spend in prayer, help us to grow in faith, hope and love.

For the End of the Primary School Year

God our Father, thank you for all the teachers who work to make our school a safe, happy and caring place in which to learn. We give thanks in this Mass for their guidance and support. Bless them always and keep them close in your love.

God our Father, you give us our parents to love and care for us. Through them, we come to know how much you love and care for us. Bless them always and keep them close in your love.

God our Father, we ask you to bless Fr N., who visited our school during the year. We give thanks for the many ways in which he helped all of us to come to know you. Bless him and his priestly work in the parish.

God our Father, we ask you to bless us, the sixth class students, as we leave our school. May we always value the gifts of friendship, care and compassion. May we always be sensitive to the needs of others.

Taken from http://www.dioceseofkerry.ie/media/uploads/End%20 of%20School%20Year%20Mass.pdf; accessed 27 August 2013.

We pray for all our young people present who are about to begin a new chapter of their lives. We pray for each of them and ask the Lord to carry them safely and happily through this transitional time and guide them to be strong in their faith and in the love of God and their parents and guardians.

Each one of these young people has their own unique personality and gifts. We ask you, Lord, to deepen their appreciation of their good points and develop independence in their worth under the guidance of their parents, guardians, teachers and community members who are willing to continue to care for them. Help our children to turn to this well of community support as they mature into fine young people in the years ahead.

We remember the grandparents of these young people, who have given such example and love to all here present since birth. Lord, bless them and give them health to continue to live well and happily as they enjoy their grandchildren in the teenage years ahead. May our young people continue to trust the wisdom of their years as they continue to respect their life experience in the ups and downs of the passing years.

We pray that the gifts of the Spirit received recently in their Confirmation will be felt by each young person here as they embark upon their secondary school years. May they be mindful of each of those gifts and turn to you morning and evening to support them as they continue to pray to you and experience your presence to them.

For Confirmation Enrolment

We ask God for the gift of understanding. May we always be kind and aware of what other people may be going through in their lives.

We ask God for the gift of wisdom. May we be wise and learn from our own life's experience.

We ask God for the gift of courage. May we always be brave and do what Jesus would want us to do.

We ask God for the gift of right judgement. May we always make the decision to stand up for what is good and just.

We ask God for the gift of reverence. May we always show respect to the people we meet, the places we go to and the things we have.

We pray for the gift of knowledge. May we always be able to use this gift to the best of our ability and know that God will always love us.

We pray for the gift of wonder and awe. May we never lose that sense of wonder of God's creation and be thankful everyday for God's presence.

For the Beginning of the Secondary School Year

We pray for all students who begin this new year of learning. May God grant us the grace and wisdom we need as we begin this new term.

We pray for all parents and guardians. May God continue to support them and encourage them to be a great example to their families.

We pray for all teachers and staff. May they share their knowledge and wisdom in a spirit of reverence and patience.

We pray for all who are under terrible financial worry and strain that may affect their child's right to education. May they receive the support and may their burdens be lifted from them.

We pray for all who struggle with school life and study. May they receive encouragement and support.

We remember all who have died, especially members of our families, teachers, staff and past pupils. May they come to the fullness of life in the presence of God.

For First Years in Secondary School

We pray for the gift of friendship and that we will be firm friends and supporters of each other as we set forth on this exciting journey. We pray for a good year. May we be honest, kind, supportive and helpful to one another.

We pray that the gifts of the Holy Spirit – wisdom, understanding, wonder and awe in God's presence – which we received in our Confirmation earlier this year will now be put into practice.

We pray for our parents and guardians who have helped us along the way. May we always show them respect and gratitude and may we show the same respect and gratitude to our teachers.

We pray for all students who may be feeling anxious at this moment. May we be sensitive to one another and be mindful of those who might need our support and friendship.

We thank God for bringing us together for the beginning of this school year and the beginning of our secondary school life.

(By Anne Rogers)

For the End of the Secondary School Year

We pray that the Holy Spirit will guide us and continue to develop our relationship with God.

May we always turn to God to seek help with the difficulties and decisions we will meet in our time apart.

May we always remember how unique and important each one of us is and that we are responsible for ourselves and the consequences of our actions.

We pray for our friends. May we always realise the importance of being a good friend and the good support that friends give.

We pray for our parents and families, and thank God for their patience, support and love.

We pray for our teachers and all in the school who have helped us grow, develop and learn.

Adapted from *Liturgies for Post-Primary Schools* by Brendan Quinlivan (Veritas, 2003).

For Exams

We pray for all students who start their exams today. May God grant them the gifts and graces they need to help them during the days ahead.

We pray that all students will use their gifts of wisdom and understanding.

We pray for all who are anxious. May they know the peace of God and recognise this in their time of need.

We pray for all students who have worked hard and to the best of their ability. May they be rewarded and trust in what will be right for them.

We pray for the families who have supported the students. May God bless them.

We pray for all who supervise and correct exams. May they be fair and honest.

We pray for students who have died, and also for students who are unable to sit their exams at this point in time. May God protect them and bless them.

Stations

We pray for everyone gathered here today. May God bless and protect this community.

We pray for all the people who helped prepare for this Station, from the painting, decorating and cleaning to the shopping and baking. May God bless you for your kindness.

We pray that the tradition of Station Masses continues, and may the message of Christ be vibrant and strong in all communities.

We pray that during this seasonal time [e.g. spring/harvest], we may be blessed with new growth and renewal.

We pray for all the children growing up in this community. May their gifts and talents be nurtured and reach their full potential.

We pray for all the members of our community who are lonely, sad or depressed. May we as their neighbours take on the Gospel call to look out for them with compassion and care.

We pray for all the members of our community who are no longer with us, especially … May God grant them everlasting peace and happiness.

General Intercessions

General

We pray for all who spread the Gospel. May the hearts of all to whom they preach be opened to receive the Word of God.

We pray for those who govern. May their policies be directed to what is good and based on justice and peace.

We pray for all present here today. May the love of Christ inspire them, the peace of Christ be with them and the strength of Christ protect them.

We pray for peace, that those parts of the world full of bloodshed and violence may experience peace and harmony.

We pray for all who have died. May they be raised to new life in the house of God.

For the Church

We pray for the whole Church: that all who follow Christ will be faithful in word and in deed.

We pray for the Church: that it will inspire all its members to make the love of God the foundation of their lives.

We pray for the members of our Church who work to spread the good news of Christ: may they do so with joy and may their message bring hope to all who hear it.

We pray for the Church: that it may present the caring, compassionate face of God to the world.

We pray for the leaders of our Church: that they may have the wisdom and vision to lead us in the footsteps of Christ.

We pray for the Church: that it will continue to faithfully proclaim the Gospel of Christ especially to those who need it most.

For Christian Unity

We pray for the unity of the Body of Christ, and that we may be freed from our sins of prejudice and intolerance. Give us a new heart, put a new spirit in us, so that we may recognise you as our God, and live in harmony with one another as your people.

We pray for peace and reconciliation between people of all Churches.

We pray for all those in ministry. May God grant them integrity of life and tenderness of heart.

We pray for peace. Help us in all our various capacities to build bridges that unite and not barriers that divide.

We pray that the divisions in society and discord between nations will no longer pose a threat to the very existence of civilisation. May the world be enlightened by your truth and transformed by your grace, so justice and peace will prevail.

We pray for industrial peace, especially in our own country, that workers and employers may treat each other with dignity and respect and work together for the common good of all our people.

We pray for God's healing touch and ask God to help us calm the anger and bitterness which can divide and alienate, and help us to forgive and heal the past, so that we can begin to create a future of justice, love and peace.

Adapted from *The Prayer of the Faithful for Weekdays*, edited by Eltin Griffin OCarm (Dominican Publications, 1985).

For Before Meetings

We pray for the courage to enter into this moment in time, into this gathering of your disciples, into this time of grace.

We pray for the courage to enter into the possibilities that lie before us, the shells on the seashore, waiting to be discovered.

We pray for the courage to enter into tasks and challenges before us, in a spirit of exploration and generosity, in the spirit of your son.

We pray for the courage to enter into the ideas and suggestions to be voiced and to hear them with an open, receptive ear, alive to the wisdom they contain.

We pray for the courage to enter into your presence, to abide in you, to be carried along by your power, reaching out to save us.

For the Environment

We pray that we may always be stewards of the earth and not masters, and that we may care for and protect the magnificence of creation.

We pray that we take time to wonder, at the sound of a bird or the scent of a flower. May we respect and value their significance.

We pray for countries where running water is so scarce. May we never waste it, pollute it or take it for granted.

We pray that all leaders and governments will put proper policies in place that will help protect our natural world.

We pray that all will be educated and converted to see the value of our planet. May they grow in knowledge, love and respect for all of nature.

For New Drivers

We pray that all who use vehicles may always be conscious of their responsibility towards others.

We pray that all danger and accidents be avoided. May we fulfil our role of responsibility and carefulness.

We pray for all who have had terrible accidents. May God bless and protect them and give them courage and strength.

We pray for all people caring for loved ones who have been badly hurt and injured. May God give them the gift of courage and may they never lose sight of their faith and trust in God.

We pray for all who have died as a result of an accident on the road. We pray for them and their grieving families.

We pray for all who travel. May God protect us in our travels and bring us safely home.

For the Alleviation of Stress

We pray for God's healing touch for the people we know who are sick or worried. We ask God to bring them peace and healing.

We pray for peace in our world, especially in countries where war and violence reign.

We pray for all who cannot sleep and are upset tonight – bring them courage and strength in their suffering and distress.

We pray that we will work to make a difference in the world, a difference that will be remembered long after we are gone.

We pray for all who were once part of our lives. We pray that they are now in God's kingdom of light, happiness and peace.

We pray for all our loved ones and for the faithful departed, especially those who have died unremembered.

For a New Home

We pray for the N.s and for their new home. May this home shelter them with God's love and blessings.

We pray for all who have helped make this new home possible in every way.

We pray that this new home be a place of welcome to all. May God's love and grace always be the welcomed guest.

We pray that this home be always safe and may it be a place where you can be who you are called by God to be.

We pray that this home and all the people who visit be examples of God's gracious invitation of love that is offered to us.

We pray that sickness and suffering will not be part of this new home. May God's grace, protection and strength always be part of this home.

For John Paul II

John Paul II worked tirelessly to promote the dignity and freedom of each person, and to bring an end to division and oppression. May we continue that mission.

John Paul II reached out to the different faiths and people of the world. May we be open to recognising the people of God as our brother or sister.

John Paul II forgave the man who tried to kill him. May we all continue his work for peace and reconciliation in our homes, communities and world.

John Paul II had a special place in his heart for young people. May our young people be inspired by his example to follow the Gospel with courage and conviction.

John Paul II suffered with his health. May his faith and courage strengthen and encourage all those who carry heavy burdens.

We pray for John Paul II himself, that he may now come to share in the risen life of Christ.

For John XXIII

We pray for John XXIII, one of the most influential popes in the history of the Catholic Church. May his legacy continue to inspire all Christian leaders throughout the world.

John XXIII was known as the 'Good Pope' for his affinity with everyone, especially prisoners and the sick. May this inspire us to continue working for the most vulnerable of our society.

John XXIII was a great communicator. With great courage and humility he reached out to all types of people. May we never be afraid to do likewise and be open to recognise everyone as our neighbour.

One of John XXIII's finest acts was the convening of the Second Vatican Council, a defining moment in Church history. May we continue to bring the vision of Vatican II to the 'people of God' in our time.

John XXIII reached out to representatives of other Christian groups. May we always remember how important this is and continue to work for peace and reconciliation in our Church.

Christianity for John XXIII was a way of living in communion with the love of God. May we always try to live in communion with the love of God.

We pray that John XXIII will continue to intercede in our prayers and may God continue to bless him.

Closing Prayers

Father in heaven, you are full of mercy and invite the poor and marginalised to your banquet. Grant us what we need today.

Father in heaven, you created the world to be a place where all people can flourish. Hear our prayers today and grant us what we need.

Heavenly Father, you cared for the people of Israel in the desert. Hear the prayers we make today and grant us what we need.

Father in heaven, you raise up the lowly and you care for the poor and the needy. Grant us what we need today.

Heavenly Father, you love justice and protect the stranger. Grant us what we need today.

God our Father, you teach us to ask, to seek, to knock at your door. In our every need, grant us the first and best of all your gifts, the Holy Spirit who makes us your children.

Father in heaven, you have shown your salvation to the nations. Hear the prayers we make today and grant us what we need.

Father, you sent your Son among us as a missionary to reveal your wonderful plan of salvation. Through our sharing of the gifts you give us, may we continue to grow in communion with our brothers and sisters throughout the world.

All prayers, unless otherwise cited, by Pamela McLoughlin, Veritas. With thanks to Anne Rogers and Sr Chris Hegarty for their compositions, and to the diocese of Kerry and the parishes of Ballyroan and Kingscourt for their permission to reproduce the prayers as cited. Acknowledgement given to the parish of Clontarf, St Oliver's Primary School, Carlingford, and Le Chéile Trust for the reproduction of prayers originally found on their websites, and to *The Prayer of the Faithful for Weekdays*, edited by Eltin Griffin OCarm and published by Dominican Publications.